Communities Around the World

Durban
South Africa

Elspeth Leacock

PICTURE CREDITS
Cover, page 23 Gallo Images/Corbis; cover (inset) Eric Wheater/Lonely Planet Images; pages 1, 2 (bottom),
15 (top) Roger De La Harpe/Gallo Images/Corbis; pages 2 (top), 8–9 (bottom), 10 (top and bottom), 15 (bottom)
Charles O'Rear/Corbis; page 3 Stone/Getty Images; pages 4, 12 (top), 14 (left and right), 15 (bottom), 16 (top)
Nik Wheeler/Corbis; pages 5, 22 (left) Peter Turnley/Corbis; page 6 (top) Michael S. Lewis/Corbis; page 6
(bottom) Chris Van Lennep, Gallo Images/Corbis; page 8 The Image Bank/Getty; page 9 (top) Courtesy/Chicago
Sister Cities; page 9 (top background) Magellan Graphix/PictureQuest; page 9 (bottom) James L. Amos/Corbis;
page 11 (top) Richard I'Anson/Lonely Planet Images; page 11 (bottom) Dave G. Houser/Corbis; pages 12–13
taxi/Getty Images; page 13 (right) Rick Gerharter/Lonely Planet Images; page 16 (bottom) AFP/Corbis; pages
17, 22 (right) AP/Wide World Photos; pages 17 (inset), 19 David Turnley/Corbis; page 18 Carl and Ann Purcell/
Corbis; page 20 Kuus/Sipa Press/Woodfin Camp and Associates, Inc.; page 21 (left) Anthony Bannister,
Gallo Images/Corbis; page 21 (right) Nubar Alexanian/Corbis; page 24 Peter Johnson/Corbis.

Maps:
Dave Stevenson

Produced through the worldwide resources of the National Geographic Society, John M. Fahey, Jr., President
and Chief Executive Officer; Gilbert M. Grosvenor, Chairman of the Board; Nina D. Hoffman, Executive Vice
President and President, Books and School Publishing.

PREPARED BY NATIONAL GEOGRAPHIC SCHOOL PUBLISHING
Ericka Markman, Senior Vice President; Steve Mico, Vice President, Editorial Director; Marianne Hiland,
Editorial Manager; Jim Hiscott, Design Manager; Kristin Hanneman, Illustrations Manager; Matt Wascavage,
Manager of Publishing Services; Sean Philpotts, Production Manager.

Production: Clifton M. Brown III, Manufacturing and Quality Control

PROGRAM DEVELOPMENT
Gare Thompson Associates, Inc.

BOOK DEVELOPMENT
Thomas Nieman, Inc.

CONSULTANTS/REVIEWERS
Dr. Margit E. McGuire, School of Education, Seattle University, Seattle, Washington
Judy Mann, Education Manager, Sea World Education Centre, Durban

BOOK DESIGN
Steven Curtis Design, Inc.

Published by the National Geographic Society
1145 17th Street, N.W.
Washington, D.C. 20036–4688

ISBN: 0-7922-8612-X

Third Printing July 2004
Printed in Canada

Durb

Table of Contents

Open-air market near
Durban's city hall

Welcome to Durban,

a community in South Africa. Hi! Or, as South Africa's Zulu people say, "Sawubona!" (sow–BAWN–uh). Read that again, out loud. You are saying "Hello" in Zulu. Zulu is one of many languages spoken in South Africa.

First, I'll show you where Durban is. Then we'll see why trade is important to us here, and what brings visitors to Durban.

Then I'll show you around the city. One thing that makes Durban special is that its people are diverse. That means you will see lots of different people and different ways of doing things.

I also want to tell you about my own people, the **Zulu**. We'll visit my cousin's village to learn about traditional Zulu ways. Then you'll enjoy a special Zulu celebration. Let's get started!

My name is Jabulani. I live here in Durban, and I would like you to come and visit.

Where Land Meets Ocean

A Place Full of Life

Durban is in the country of South Africa. As you might guess, South Africa is in the southern part of the **continent** of Africa. So, to find Durban you must first go to the southern tip of Africa. Now can you find Durban? It is on the southeastern coast where the African land meets the Indian Ocean.

South Africa has a warm, sunny **climate.** Because of this, many different kinds of beautiful flowers grow here. We have some strange looking plants too. There is the **baobab** tree. Our storytellers say that, as a joke, the gods put this tree on the earth upside down! (Check out page 23 and you'll see why.)

A lot of animals like our climate too. You can see elephants, giraffes, crocodiles, and many more animals in South Africa's zoos and **game reserves.**

Weather Report

Forecast: Sunny

If you like sunshine, you will love the climate here in Durban! The sun shines about 320 days a year. It is hot and humid during the summer months. But even in winter, it is still warm enough to go swimming. Do you know what the **equator** is? It's an imaginary line running around the earth halfway between the North and South Poles. Since Durban is south of the equator, June, July, and August are our winter. That means that Christmas comes during summer vacation!

Surfing at Durban

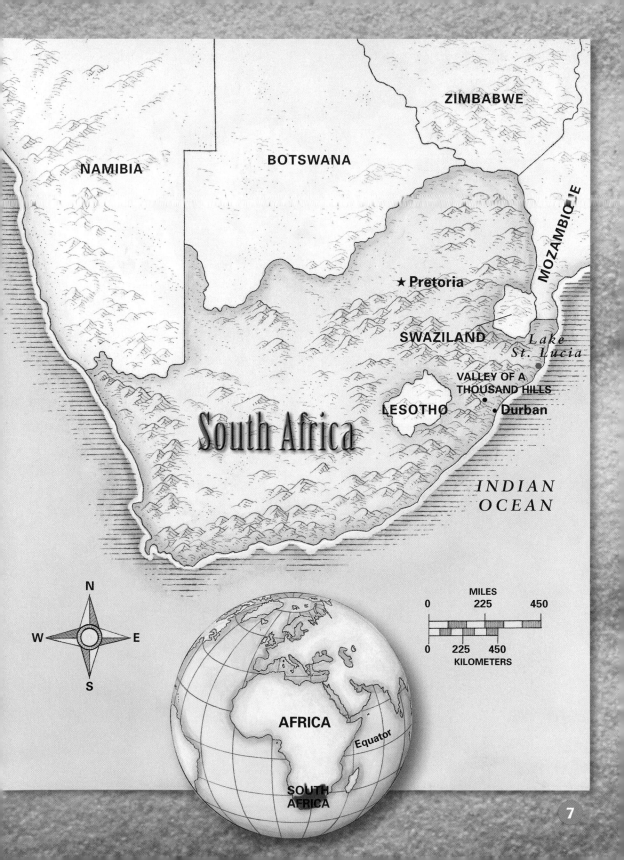

ZIMBABWE

NAMIBIA

BOTSWANA

MOZAMBIQUE

★ Pretoria

SWAZILAND

Lake
St. Lucia

VALLEY OF A
THOUSAND HILLS

LESOTHO

• Durban

South Africa

INDIAN
OCEAN

N
W   E
S

MILES
0   225   450

0   225   450
KILOMETERS

AFRICA

Equator

SOUTH
AFRICA

A Safe Place for Ships

Durban grew into a city because it has a good harbor. A harbor is a safe place for ships. In 1497, an explorer from Portugal named Vasco da Gama was sailing around southern Africa. On Christmas Day, he sighted the coast where Durban is today. He called the place "Natal" from the Portuguese word for "Christmas." In 1823, an English ship came to our harbor to find shelter from a terrible storm. The English decided to start a settlement here.

My people, the Zulus, were here already. They had come from the north long ago. The part of South Africa where Durban is located is called KwaZulu-Natal today. KwaZulu means "Place of the Zulu." The Zulus traded animal skins and ivory with the English. Soon, many ships were coming here bringing goods to trade.

Ships in the Indian Ocean near Durban

In the 1860s, South Africa began to produce a lot of sugar. Many people came to Durban from India to work in the sugar industry. Other Indians came here to trade. Both the sugar industry and the Indian traders helped the port of Durban grow. And these Indians became part of the people of Durban.

Today, Durban is the biggest port in all of Africa. More than 5,000 ships come here every year. We are lucky to be located near the great shipping lanes. They are like highways for boats on the ocean. My dad says that means that our port gets a lot of traffic, and that is good for business.

Here and There

Sister City

Durban has a "sister city." It is Chicago, Illinois. Chicago is not next to the ocean like Durban is. But it is on Lake Michigan, one of the Great Lakes. So, like Durban, Chicago is a port city where goods are loaded and unloaded from boats and trains. Both cities are located where shipping lanes and railroad lines meet. So, in important ways Chicago and Durban are the same, like sisters.

Cargo ship at Chicago

A Center for Trade

Who makes Durban such a busy port? Who **exports** our goods by sending them to other places? Who **imports** the things that we want but don't grow or make here? Do you know? Well, **merchants** do! Let's go visit one of Durban's merchants.

Her name is Chandrika Haribhai. Her great-grandfather came from India to Durban many years ago and started a small shop. Now Haribhai's spice store covers a whole city block near the harbor. It is the biggest spice market in all of South Africa. Did you ever see so many spices in your whole life? Just standing in this store is like a feast for your eyes, and your nose too. I love the smells here.

A Durban spice shop

Do you know where all of these goods come from? The spices are mostly imported from India, the almonds are from California, the dates come from Saudi Arabia, and the pistachios from Iran. Nearly everything here is imported.

Farmers keep the port busy too. Farmers around Durban grow lots of bananas and sugar cane. You know what's made from sugar cane, right? Sugar! So much sugar is exported from Durban that there is a huge terminal at the port just for loading boats with sugar. Durban is the biggest sugar port in the world today.

What else does Durban ship besides sugar? Well, there are many things, including wood chips (for making paper), rice, citrus products, coal, steel, and chemicals. But Durban's harbor is not just a place for work. There is also a passenger boat terminal where people on vacation come and go. People having fun also help make Durban a busy port.

Sugar cane fields and farming village near Durban

Sugar cane harvest

A Great Place to Visit

Lots of people come here for vacations. They come for our sunny climate and beautiful sandy beaches. And that is not all. Let's see why Durban is so popular.

First stop is the "Golden Mile." That's what we call one of our beautiful sandy beaches on the Indian Ocean. You can surf, sailboard, or swim here. There are water slides, fountains to play in, and places to eat. People enjoy the warm sun, sand, and water. And they don't have to worry about the sharks here. There are nets in the water that keep them away.

If you want to see some sharks, you can go to Sea World. I like to go at feeding time. There are dolphin shows too. Do you like snakes?

If you do, there is Snake Park. There are 80 different kinds of snakes there as well as some big bad crocodiles. Scary, huh?

When you have had enough sun and surf we can follow the tourists and board a bus to some of the game reserves. You can shoot an elephant or a rhino! Not with a gun of course. You can shoot pictures with a camera!

Up the coast is Lake St. Lucia. Don't think of going swimming here. The water is teeming with crocodiles. There are lots of hippos too. Many people think that hippos are gentle, but they're not. These huge creatures kill more people than any other large mammal in Africa! Always listen to the guides. They will keep you safe.

Rickshaws

One way to get around in Durban's beachfront is to take a rickshaw. A rickshaw is a small, two-wheeled carriage pulled by a driver. Rickshaw drivers dress in the most fantastic outfits for the tourists. Look at this one! He won't try to run with that headdress on. It's only for pictures.

One of Durban's rickshaw drivers

Rhinos in a game reserve

CHAPTER 2
All Around Durban

A Diverse City

Today we are going to see how the people of Durban live. Like any big city, Durban has very different neighborhoods—rich and poor and in-between. As you look around, you can see that the city is diverse, but the neighborhoods are less so. That is because in the past there was something called **apartheid.**

Apartheid (uh–PART–hyt) means "apartness," and for many years different groups—white people, Africans, and Indians—were kept apart from each other. It was against the law for people of these different groups to live in the same neighborhoods. They could not share schools. They could not share the beautiful beaches. Their children couldn't even play with each other! But that is all changing. Now it is apartheid that is against the law. And this is a good thing!

Jumah Mosque

14

Durban's different groups of people worship in different ways. Many Africans and Indians are **Muslims**. Muslims worship at a **mosque**. Durban's Jumah Mosque is one of the largest in the world. Many other Indians are **Hindus**. There are beautiful Hindu temples here in Durban. There are also churches for Durban's many Christians.

Hindu wedding

Downtown Durban street

"Unity is Strength"

This is the motto in South Africa now. You can see that idea everywhere. Even in the new flag that flies in front of City Hall. The flag has stripes of many different colors, but they all come together. This reminds all of us to come together and work as one.

Our new flag was first raised on April 27, 1994. My mom and dad said that they cried for joy when they saw it. That day was the very first time that all South Africa's people could vote. Around Durban, thousands of Zulu people lined up and stood in the hot sun for hours and hours and hours to cast their ballots.

A man named Nelson Mandela was a big part of this change. Under apartheid, he was sent to prison for life. But people and governments around the world protested. Finally, after 27 long years, he was freed. And remember that first great election day when all South Africans could vote? Well, the result was Nelson Mandela became South Africa's first black president!

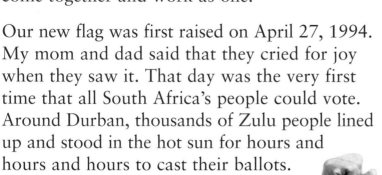

Nelson Mandela

South Africans waiting in line to vote

Young poll worker helping an elderly voter

17

CHAPTER 3

Friends and Family

A Day in the Country

Today we are going to visit my cousin, Mandla.
We drive away from the city and out to the
countryside. This place is called the Valley of a
Thousand Hills. This is where Mandla lives. After
the buzz of Durban, it is so quiet. Listen! You can
hear the tinkle of cowbells as boys herd their
fathers' cattle into pens for the night.

Some of the homes have round mud walls baked
by the sun. They are nice and cool in the summer.
Other homes are made of concrete with tin roofs.
Long ago, Zulus built beautiful homes that
looked just like beehives. I love the old homes,
but they are hard to find now.

Zulu homes are small and simple inside. But in
a climate like this, why stay inside? Most people
here do just about everything outside, even their
cooking. Which reminds me, I hope that you're
hungry. Mandla's family is fixing a barbecue.

Young Zulu herding
his father's cattle

Shaka's Day

This is a special day for the Zulu people.
Thousands of people gather to honor a great warrior king named Shaka Zulu. He ruled a Zulu empire long ago. But he was so powerful that he is remembered to this day. He is one of my heroes. For most Zulu people, this is a day to honor and remember Shaka Zulu and our roots.

Zulus who live in the country, like my cousin's family, make a special effort. Nearly everybody wears traditional Zulu dress. The men wear beautiful skins and feathers. They carry spears and large cowhide shields. They look the way Shaka Zulu's warriors looked long ago.

There are long speeches. But there is dancing and music and good food too. And there's lots of time to visit with friends. Listen and you will hear the poets sing the praises of Shaka Zulu. The present Zulu king is also honored. He is dressed in skins today too. But don't think that's how he dresses all the time. He is a modern king, so he usually wears a suit.

Statue of Shaka Zulu

Zulu Singers

Ladysmith Black Mambazo is the name of my favorite Zulu singing group. It was founded by in the 1960s by Joseph Shabalala. The group began as a choir of nine boys. They had no musical instruments. The music was just their voices. They are the same today except they are no longer boys! Now they are men, and they tour around the world, even in the USA. They won a Grammy Award for their first album there, "Shaka Zulu."

Joseph Shabalala with Zulu dancers

Dancers in a Zulu village

At School

Welcome to my school. I began school by speaking Zulu. Then I learned English. Next I learned some **Afrikaans.** Afrikaans is the language of Dutch people who settled in South Africa hundreds of years ago. There are 11 official languages in South Africa. Most South Africans learn at least three of them. Learning all of these languages is a lot of work. But we still have time for math and science and geography too, just like you.

We also take field trips and learn about nature. When I grow up I want to work at one of the game reserves like my dad. But I love sports too. Sometimes I dream of playing soccer for my country in the Olympics! I need to practice.

Good-bye for now, or "Hamba Kahle" (hum–bah kah–leh), as Zulus say.

Soccer in Four Languages!

People here in South Africa learn languages outside school too. When I turn on the television to watch a soccer game, a sportscaster gives the exciting, play-by-play description in Zulu for 15 minutes.

The next 15 minutes will be in **Xhosa** (KOH–sah). Then there will be 15 minutes in English. And the last 15 minutes will be in another of South Africa's 11 languages. I can hear and learn 4 languages just by tuning in to watch my favorite team play!

Soccer players

Glossary

Afrikaans   language of Dutch settlers of South Africa

apartheid   system of laws that forced South Africa's different peoples to live apart from one another

baobab   a tree of tropical Africa

climate   the pattern of weather in an area

continent   one of the seven biggest bodies of land on earth—Africa, Antarctica, Asia, Australia, Europe, North America, and South America

equator   an imaginary circle around the earth, halfway between the North Pole and the South Pole

export   to send goods to other countries

game reserve   area in which animals in the wild are protected

Hindu   a believer in Hinduism, traditional religion of India

import   to bring goods from another country

merchant   a person who buys and sells goods for a living

mosque   a Muslim place of worship

Muslim   a believer in Islam, the religion founded by Muhammad

Xhosa   the language of a people native to South Africa

Zulu   a people native to South Africa and their language

Baobab tree

Index